Notes From Beulah

Katelyn Mattson

Copyright © 2024 by Katelyn Mattson

All rights reserved.

No portion of this book may be reproduced in any form without written permission from the publisher or author, except as permitted by U.S. copyright law.

To Shepard, Miriam, and Georgina. I hope this book finds its way onto the bookshelves of your grandchildren. Thank you to everyone in my life who has shown me what love looks like: my children, my dear parents and siblings, my fierce girlfriends, and JWK. Thank you to my editor, Katy Lindhart, and to all of YOU for bearing witness to a year in my life.

This collection contains poetry written between July 2023 – July 2024.

Prologue
Take It 1

Act I
The Mystic 2
Hacksaw Jim Duggan 3
Dichotomies 4
You 5
Fall 6
Momentary 7
Love 8
The Writer 9
Baptism 10
Saturday 11
Last Supper 12
Quail Egg 13
The Unprecedented 14
Two Lovers Over Breakfast 15
Crash Landing 16
Tu me manques 17
Fine China 18
As Easy as Pie 19

Act II
I Will Wait for You 20
Come Back 21
Five Months 22
Unfortunate Fruit 23
How is Your Healing 24
Food Pantry 25
Men 26
Autopsy 27
RIP to My Therapy Journal 28

Path of Totality 29
Shame 30
Into the Ground 31
Timed Mile 32
How Many Times 33
Stitch My Rage 34
Gone Fishin' 35

Act III
Tomato Sandwiches 36
Solitude 37
Aurora 38
To My Younger Self 39
Romanticize Your Life 40
June 41
Solstice 42
I am Magic 43
Get Witchy with Me 44
The Comment Section 45
Bubblegum Pink 46
Limitless 47
I'd Like to Thank My Delusion 48
Mother of Girls 49
I've Got You 50
Alice 51
Alice #2 52
All is Well 53
Different Lives 54
One Year Sober 55
Basement Floor 56
Main Character 57

Epilogue
When I am Gone 58

Prologue

Take It

what do I do with all this love
oozing through the barrier of my skin
i could scoop it up with bare hands
like water through sealed fingers
and make chicken soup for my neighbor

let it overflow out into the darkness
anyone who needs a light can follow me
until we find what they've lost
i know you put it somewhere easy to remember
some days we forget the important places

it feels unjust to keep it to myself
take it
i've plenty to spare
i've been in need before and found a river
flowing from strangers through city streets

Act I

The Mystic

A mystic told me I've yet to meet my greatest love
It's been months now and I still try to manifest you
I tied a note with red string and sent it down a river

Hacksaw Jim Duggan

Has love ever struck you upside the head?
Like Hacksaw Jim Duggan on a Saturday morning

It happened and my head still hurts
I was walking down the hall
Following the smell of his skin
He was church, a benediction, my peace

It blew me over
Knowing it would either be the last love of my life
Or leave me wishing it were

We were sitting in a symphony hall
His hungry hands in my skirt
My desperate heart in his hands
I blamed my tears on Mozart

I didn't die but stopped going to church
Now I watch wrestling every Saturday
Dreaming of who's next

Dichotomies

Sweet dichotomies
Two different experiences of the same love
Will I ever stop feeling a fool?
Will I ever stop hoping you'll darken my door again?

You

Looking at you looking at me
Everything you say is obvious
Of course

This is it, isn't it?
The sweet spot
That itch between shoulder blades
The cool side of a pillow
Walking down an autumn road
A bit that never dies

I'll build a home in this spot
Where giddiness morphs into aching
And discovering you might as well be a moon landing

Fall

I've always wanted to fall in love in October
Fall is a renaissance for our souls
A brave branch turning orange
Mist on warm ground eager for change

My skin is tight
Aching for the scent of earth and fire
Move in this season of warmth with me
We will head toward the promise of change
Dancing barefoot on a blanket of leaves

Momentary

I have a plan
And it isn't all good
I'm going to binge on your obsession
And your momentary rapture
Will heal my heart

Perhaps I'll put a spell on your tongue
It will list in scrumptious detail
All the ways I am your unique and unrepeatable beauty
You'll swear eternal devotion to this belly
Plum with decades of hate
Using that tongue to prove it

Your hands have a full agenda
Start by washing my feet
Spend time browsing the inventory of my thighs
Magnetic hands unable to break free
It's just chemistry, I tell myself
Refusing to put any hope in tomorrow
Move in
I've cleared a drawer and hope you leave a tribute
Lay your cheek on my heart
Breathe in my existence
This moment in time will feed me for a decade

Love

Sometimes love is as big
As watching your mother meet her first grandbaby
Most of the time it's as big
As finding the perfect pen and knowing exactly who to tell

The Writer

I always knew I'd fall in love with a writer
He'd compose poems about my hips
Recite prose between my thighs
Pinch me
Not too hard
In case this is a dream

Baptism

Let me trace the roadmap of your veins with my tongue
I'm on edge from them
Your rivers of strength - of vitality

I'll start with your right arm
Streams tickling down from the mountains
Joining together to form a Moldau
A life source

Down it swirls into your fingertips
Whose icy water quenches my thirst
I do believe I will love you
Drink from you
Bathe in you
Baptize me

Saturday

Another Saturday
The mundane dancing with profound
There is a rotting rotisserie in the fridge
And two loads of linens wrinkling on the table

Forget chicken and laundry
For 24 hours I am yours and you are mine

Last Supper

I am seasoned with your obsession
Spicy
Earthy
Nutty
Salty
I am the bread of life
Enjoy your last supper

Quail Egg

Our love is old-fashioned
A delicate crocheted doily on the back of a chair
Sweet tea on the wraparound porch of a corner house
Chipped paint and open windows

My soul held with such tenderness
You'd think it a quail egg
Devoted and unyielding

Time is measured in throaty sighs
Counted as tally marks on our hearts
We unzip our skin and crawl inside caverns of peace
We never understand how weary we are
Until finding someone to rest in

The Unprecedented

I wish you a wealth of unprecedented days

An extra five dollars for fancy cheese
Eaten wearing yesterday's socks
Your next read shelved five minutes
Before swinging open the old library door
A love who lies beside you as you nap
Even when they aren't tired
The kind wave of a stranger at a four-way stop

Imagine days so stunningly beige
That shimmers of beauty make it above the fold
I once dreamed of headlines
Now I dream of softness

My children cuddled in my bed telling secrets
The sound and scent of a waking kitchen
Helping someone till they find their next paycheck
Sharing music when words lose all meaning

The softness of the unprecedented is extraordinary
I wish us all a wealth of unprecedented days

Two Lovers Over Breakfast

We are two lovers in a breakfast nook
I study how you rest in my chair
Buttering your sourdough
Complimenting my bacon
                Perfectly cooked, my love
You take turns nibbling on toast and my fingertips
Teasing me with your new tattoo
Seductively peeking out underneath your cotton shirt
                I love you so much, it says
Purring like kittens in a sunbeam
We scoot closer and sigh at our profound joy
The smell of burnt bacon lingers in the air

Crash Landing

sometimes i smell you in a room of strangers
they say to secure your mask before helping others
i wish i could inhale you as we crash land

Tu me manques

I was happiest attended to by your obsession
Innately selfish
Wanting to be your everything
Your limerent object

I paced barefoot at my door
Waiting for your late arrival
Grounding myself to anything tangible

Hoist me upon a marble pedestal
Kiss my feet covered in earth

My desperation comes from decades of rotting hearts
Blind to my strange beauty
Repelled by my intensity and fire

But you
You lived for me and I took a life
Lock me behind bars
Throw the key into an ocean

Fine China

I painted your heartbeat in oils
Composed odes to your veins
If memory serves
                my memory serves up a feast
You declared allegiance to my body
Damming God and every cunt that came before mine
          your memory eats at my table
I will keep a place setting for you
bowls of chipped clay and wood
Our love was earthy
              the soil holds memories for centuries

As Easy as Pie

My love is a banquet
Croissants and key lime pie
Taste me and feast

Remember how your name slipped from my lips
As easy as pie
Let the salt and sweet linger on your tongue
I will spoil soon enough

Act II

I Will Wait for You

And if one morning
A crow brings a silver button to my door
I'll know it traveled from your favorite grey suit
No doubt it finally had enough
And cast itself away
A message in a bottle, sent with a prayer.

I've seen many trinkets left as offerings
Elastic bands and shiny pebbles
A tiny gold key and feathers
An engagement ring
All traveling from faraway places by determined beaks
I place them in a wooden box
With deepest appreciation
For the adventures they've seen

And if one morning
A crow brings a silver button from your favorite grey suit
I'll give it a place of honor on my bedside table
You'll find it next to my glass paperweight
Where it will stay until you return home

Come Back

I once thought I'd lost my most cherished ring
One day it reappeared
Resting in the exact place I swore I looked a dozen times

Perhaps we have something in common
It refuses to be owned
I imagine it out in the world
Finding its way into another's possession
For a brief moment it will be cherished
Before being lost again

They'll search everywhere before letting go
Maybe it will find its way back here
To the exact place

Five Months

Five months to the day
The last memory of your hands in my hair
I can't remember milk at the store
Yet recall your smile every morning as I pour my coffee
You walked to the ends of the earth and leapt into the abyss
Every Sunday I host the Flat Earth Society
It's filled with hearts that refuse to accept the truth
We take turns dissecting the evidence
Reassuring one another over tea that we are perfectly sane
It was real
And you are gone

Unfortunate Fruit

Look again
I'm not bruised or damaged
Nor moldy from a life crept up too soon
I am ripe and plump
Filled with juicy eternity

Yet you discarded me like unfortunate fruit
I yearn for my seeds to be plucked effortlessly
Gently cupped in a hand
Unbutton my leaves
Swear unending devotion to my scarlet flesh

Wear it like a letter upon your chest
My stain edging the contour of your lips

                I love this wilting tartness
                She tastes like sugar
                She taught me how to love
                I did her wrong
                But I keep a field of strawberries
                In the hopes I am worthy of her memory

How is Your Healing?

Does an atomic clock never break?
Let's not speak in absolutes
Be suspicious with me
In my journal lives a map
Forging out different paths
Insufferably intricate, each with a key

Last night I sat in the sunset and tapped my collarbone
Wondering if the only action here is inaction
Oscillating between doing and being

I suppose I am healing
We can thank time for that
The osmosis of a juicy life
Lessons seeping into my skin
Teaching time a thing or two
Creating a wayward compass for my future

Food Pantry

My love is a little food pantry
Perched on the side of the road
Gabled roof and turquoise paint
Take what you need and leave the rest
I'll keep it stocked with raspberry jam
And wait in a chair for your return

Men

I am a tidal wave doomed by nature
Leaving in my wake the corpses of men
Who weren't ready to love me

Autopsy

the names of those we love are tattooed on our hearts
as we lay cold on metal slabs with our chests sawed open
the autopsy room becomes a poetry slam
a gambling hall
taking bets on who made it onto the left ventricle
is the canvas of my heart big enough to continue to love?
or will it one day run out of room
perhaps that's the day it gives out

RIP to My Therapy Journal

This isn't working
Daily journals filled with wellness hacks
Copious notes from therapy
A library dedicated to books that were going to save me

What if we forget our diagnoses for a day
Leaving that unhealed trauma in a heap on the floor
Alongside our laundry
Consider the possibility
That we are healing ourselves to death
We'll put our exhausted brains into hospice
Marveling in the beauty that is living

Let's paint a mural of our gratitudes
Collect wildflowers on a prairie walk
Teach our children the value of a nap
Drink a glass of water and objectify our own bodies

Look at you, living in this body
Do you even know all the ways you're important?

Don't you see you are enough for everyone but yourself?
We're going to allow this part of us to die with dignity
Forgetting everything we've learned about being broken

Path of Totality

indigenous elders teach us to stay inside today
the sun is dying to be reborn
i trust them more than anyone
so i made a dentist appointment

choosing the mundane over once in a lifetime
i'm content with my current functional freeze
happy to pretend it's simply another day in my life

i've been told my life changes forever this afternoon
that i must be careful and not travel on the water
old boyfriends will surface
my wildest dreams will come true

how boring it will be sitting in my dentist's chair
leaving with clean teeth instead of an entirely new life
it's too early to ruminate on astrological miracles
can't today just be a Monday?

Shame

Shame pulsates in dark places
Propagating with drops of memory
It overtakes the body
Ivy breaks through mortar and stone
Cracking a foundation of peace
Robbing us of joy and hope
Progress and evolution

The quorum agrees it must be abolished
Hold my hand and I'll send in light
The sun on our faces on a February day
A baby's fist curled around a finger
Knowing smiles shared with strangers

Swap shame with your neighbor
It will die in humanity
We are more alike than you think
I, too, drink my shame in the dark

Into the Ground

See that piece of cottonwood bark?
The one covered in moss housing a family
Kick it and a dusty vape will cover us in my childhood
Forging for clarity beneath jagged memories
Each with razor blade edges

I wish I had a ghost of Christmas past
Who would lift the veil of my decades

Under a limestone brick lives all my shame
Too heavy for us to carry
Let's take turns stomping it into the dirt
Cementing all the times I knew better into the earth's core
There they'll melt — leaving no trace
Exhuming self-worth from tombs

Timed Mile

The discomfort of change
Sticky and humid
Sits before me with an inevitable confidence
I've been here before
She brings an air of terror with her into my room
Like a timed mile proctored by a butch with a stopwatch
Becoming one's true self is a painful process
Half a century old and I'm still hurting

How Many Times

How many times must I sage my fucking house
Before the remnants of every vile memory disappear

Solstice, full moon, new moon,
New Year, eclipse, Monday, Friday...
Open windows and positive intentions
I move from room to room
Erasing every generational ache

I clean my mind
Remembering how the body keeps the score
Are my traumas aligned with the cosmos?
I feel them with every shift of the planets
I feel them every Monday, Friday...

How many times must I sage this fucking house
Before it feels like home

Stitch My Rage

Rage
Often stifled beneath a tufted quilt
A four-letter word
I'll create a new pattern
Hues of dusty rose and lavender
Thick enough to put out a fire
Flammable enough to burn it all to the ground

Gone Fishin'

I wish I could hang a sign around my neck
Gone fishin'
A gentle way to let you know I am unavailable
Meant to be lighthearted
A warning with hints of whimsy

I'll be back soon

Act III

Tomato Sandwiches

I'll be back when tomato season ends
Until then imagine me standing over the sink
Right foot propped up against my left
Barefoot, braless, nightgown-ed
Crickets and cicadas
Sweat pooling and daydreams overflowing
An heirloom tomato still warm from the sun
Her juice is mixed with mayo and salt
Her life's work in my mouth

Solitude

Are you through being alone now?
Is a current surging through your bones?
New pathways set aflame in your mind
Moving one foot in front of the other

Or will you walk to the door and shove the deadbolt
Cementing another row of stone around your body
Becoming your own worst fear
The self-fulfilling prophecy you once prayed away

Aurora

Aurora came to visit last night
Bringing colors I've never seen to the night sky
Standing in the middle of a country road with my children
Each of us filled with wonder and gratitude
If the universe could bring the lights to us
Maybe there is something to be said
For standing still and waiting

To My Younger Self

The world is hungry enough as it is
Serve yourself up on a silver platter
Your purpose will be found
By sharing slices of your soul

Your spirit will be delighted food for the famished
Feed them warm rhubarb pie served à la mode
Be chalant in a world of non

Romanticize Your Life

Imagining the landscape has eyes
What would it see?

A mother and daughter on a picnic blanket
Braiding their hair and telling secrets
Slicing a mango while listening to birds

Running outside into a sudden downpour
Grabbing sheets off the line wearing muddy bare feet
Still smiling about it thirty minutes later

A loud caftan spritzed with cherry perfume
Worn while painting the sunset
Surrounded by mewing kittens
In a house that smells of sawdust

June

summer carries a different sort of romance
one that feels ripe with potential
yet slow from heat and sweat
my bedroom fan runs for three months straight
I wonder how I ever slept
without the company of her hum
find me at the river
soothed by slight rapids
and sand slipping through my toes

Solstice

To be a blueberry in summer
To live a life with one purpose:
Grow plump and be devoured
The lucky ones are enjoyed by impatient fingers
Unable to resist a berry warmed by the sun
Popping between their molars

I am Magic

my magic is grown in a greenhouse
worms feast in black soil
spicy cocktails of potent air nourish my roots
watch me cast a spell in a sunbeam
see how my essence dances in the wind
dressed as pollen and dust
blessing everything in its path
i water this soul and prune withered edges
making way for new life

my magic is grown in a greenhouse
every piece of me can be used in a ritual
take me into your body and be transformed
men love to steal bites so they can see god
hallucinating that I belong to them
tethering my heart deep into the earth with a stake
                                        "do not touch"

Get Witchy with Me

To be thought a witch is epic
The highest praise
Pagan!
Heathen!
Devil's spawn!
Oh, thank you. I try.
My ninth ancestral grandmother was called a witch
She stood trial at Salem
Accused after storming out of church
Slamming the doors on fire and brimstone
What a woman, I whisper in awe
I too have slammed the door on religion
And been known to cast a spell or two
I once manifested a great love
It didn't last so I need to check my notes
Come over on the solstice
We'll dance naked in the moonlight
Write the names of our crushes in red
And relish in our sanctuary

The Comment Section

I obsess over your love story
Reading your tender, porny comments
With the giddiness of cracking open a fortune cookie
Just a voyeur sniffing out lyrics

Bubblegum Pink

There is an invisible string
Connecting my children to my chest
It's bubblegum pink
Floating in a tepid breeze
They're a living museum
Whose history floats down woven threads
Into my heart

I remind them that they grew in me
I am yours and you are mine
My body lives in your body
My mother's past treads our water
You are imprinted in my every cell

Our bubblegum string
Holds the strength
Of the San Francisco Bridge
Lives zooming back and forth
Filled with people going, growing, gone
Yet this connection stands the test of time

When you were born I gave myself to you
Now so much of myself travels around outside my body
Come home, no matter where life takes you
I will always be here
A titan of engineering and physics

Limitless

How much love can one person take in a day
Surely there is a limit
Love rips the stitches on this heart
My day leaks out into the world around me
Making everything glisten

I'd Like to Thank My Delusion

I believe I've now grown past middle age
Closer to the grave than the cradle
Yet I still fall in love as it were the first time
My heart still swells at the sound of a Christmas carol
When I close my eyes I can smell my mama

My children don't understand
That I'm growing up with them
They expect answers
So, I give them an Oscar winning performance
Every night after I've kissed their sleepy heads
I give my acceptance speech

      "I'd like to thank my delusion
      for always pulling me through"

Mother of Girls

So much of me lives in my daughter
I see my mother in her eyes
Her room is a graveyard of my forgotten joys
Twinkle lights hung on a headboard
Colorful baubles proudly displayed
The exquisite luxury of a pink couch
Darling little dolls playing house

When did I stop delighting in girlhood?
Was it the weight of my first paycheck?
The amnesia of my first love?
I'd choose a thousand days in this room with her
Over the harshness of the world
So, I sip my tea on her pink couch
Imagining myself eleven years old

I've Got You

My mother and I shared secrets
I helped her die
The biggest secret of them all
She was done. I helped her be done.
I lit one last Salem menthol from her hidden stash
Holding it up to her lips
We shared hits, giggling
Delighting in breaking rules
Her last laugh

Tumors had broken her spine and spirit
"I don't want to live like this"

Okay, mama. I've got you.
It will be our little secret

I found another twenty packs of hidden Salems
I lit one and let out what sounded like a laugh
Although it felt like a prayer
Hiding out behind the garage
Smoking my mother's cigarettes
Silent tears of relief soaking my cheeks

Mothers and daughters spend a lifetime trading secrets
You gave me life; I gave you death

Alice

You visited my dreams
Oh, how I wish you could stay
Sit at my new kitchen table!
It hasn't the pleasure of knowing you
It hasn't the pleasure of your memory

This door remembers
All the times your hand touched its weathered wood
This stone hearth watched you grow
Porous enough to seal up the image of your childhood

This house is a memoir
Every morning I turn a page
These walls read bedtime stories
Cocooning me in strength

We are the women who came before us

Alice #2

When the frequency of our laughs synced
Entire rooms would stop and stare
The sparkle of pride in her eyes
Shone on me mischievously
The familiarity of my mother is still here
It pops up unexpectedly from time to time
In organizing files at 2 AM
And brewing coffee at 5
Oil paint under my fingernails
A whirling sea filled with secrets
How I scratch my daughter's back
And raise up my chin to look into my son's eyes
I understand my mother more everyday
And wish she still existed in the world
So I could ask

All is Well

when my parents died they took my fear with them
it's strange to miss them so deeply
think on them with such gratitude
yet feel a strange relief
two less people to make proud
thank god

i love you
everything here is well
i need to trim the hedges out front
i left my husband
would you be ashamed or relieved?
i fall in love easily now
it's more like skydiving
crashing into the ground
there was one man who so wished he could have known you
he left me without a parachute

i'm glad you're dead
you'd have to pick up the pieces
you already spent a lifetime putting me back together
i might have sent you to an early grave
so sorry
i am the middle child after all
rest well
all is well

Different Lives

We live two different lives
One before they die
One after they're gone
It's the in-between where I get lost
Between smelling them on the pillow
And the familiar slowly dying away

One Year Sober

Rest in peace, ambrosia
You darling friend
Platelets carried your tolerance throughout my body
Take it away and I bleed out
Staining everything good to ever come my way
Numbing pain from things unspoken

The Basement Floor

I lit the pilot light and had a revelation
Laying there in my dingy basement
Along with a decade of dust too inconvenient to notice

Staring up at warped wood
Wondering if my kitchen might one day fall through
The line of built-ins filled with three generations

A ceramic owl
A Stradivarius
Glass wedding ornaments in satin

My ninth ancestral grandmother was tried at Salem
I think of her everyday

We are the sum of our parts
Mine are forgotten
Covered in dust

Main Character

A man remarked on my strong sexual energy
Stroking my coffee mug like the cool, hard flesh of a lover
Breathing in peaches at the market
Fetishizing how their juice would run off my chin
Just a girl in her own world
Wondering who is peeking in

Epilogue

When I am Gone

i hope my stories collect dust
in a used bookstore in Kansas
       what will I leave behind?
a life lived wild
dreams filled with audacity
art, music, poetry
children who've only known true love
stories told for generations
at least one broken heart
slinking out of the woodwork like cockroaches after dark
throwing themselves upon my casket
       yes, make a scene
my words will walk strangers through ecstasy and grief
as if giving directions to the nearest subway
will they read my words with tears in their eyes?
discovering a soul that speaks their native tongue
my complexities are a roadmap for suffering and joy
       it's been my absolute pleasure
look for me on the top shelf
tucked away glowing in the knowing
       my life was everything I hoped it would be

Made in the USA
Columbia, SC
01 December 2024